DAILY ✠EXPRESS AND SUNDAY ✠EXPRESS

CARTOONS

FIFTY FOURTH SERIES

GILES CHARACTERS™ & © 2000 Express Newspapers

Published by

Pedigree®

The Old Rectory, Matford Lane, Exeter, Devon, EX2 4PS
Under licence from Express Newspapers
Printed in Italy. ISBN 1-902836-34-0

GI 54

An Introduction by

Dame Thora Hird

Someone once said "Take your work very seriously and yourself not at all". They were wise words and ones I have tried to follow throughout my career in the theatre - they always come back to me whenever I open a new Giles Annual. Giles took his work very seriously and the world he created laughed all traces of our famous British self importance out of the window!

You know, what I love most about a Giles cartoon is it's richness. There is so much going on! Once you have laughed at the main punchline - always so witty and cleverly observed - there are all the other hilarious things in the background. No wonder we can look at his pictures over and over again without growing tired of them.

Most important to me though, as a Northerner who likes to speak as she finds, is the clever way that Giles pokes fun at our way of life. He shows things how they really are, not how we are told they are and that is so refreshing, especially as it is always done with such affection and humour.

Being in the cast of "Last of the Summer Wine", the longest running sitcom in the history of television, I know what it is like to be part of a comic institution. Now having been asked to introduce this latest collection of classic cartoons, I feel part of another great one and it makes me proud. Thank you, Giles, for making me laugh for as long as I can remember - and that's a very long time!

Thora Hird

CONTENTS

Social

"It's for you, dear - the Editor wants to know when the something or other he's going to get a cartoon."

Shop assistants who excel in civility and skill will be eligible for a
"national certificate of retail efficiency".

"Well, I'll be glad when this strike's over - I've left my car up there."

"Well, I haven't parked it IN a street with yellow bands on the lamp posts, have I?"

"Lovely weather we're having lately, aren't we?"

"Twenty million pounds in gold for the U.S.A. - that's more than you could part with without a pinch, ain't it?"

"I don't blame Cripps for not liking 'em - you can't even sit down!"

"Are you the salesman who persuaded my neighbour to buy a thirty-valve radio
with extension speakers in every room?"

"Who are we gunning for today, grandma - imperialist warmongers or petrol snoopers?"

"I said: 'Even if we shan't be able to see him we'll still be able to hear him.'"

"If you hit my thumb many more times I'm going to forget about being as merry and bright as I'm supposed to be this week."

"I'll give you a tenner apiece for 'em."

"This is the part I like about their New Look - ironing day."

"Honest, lady, we didn't spoil your dinner - we only work 'ere."

"Etty says she ain't sure if she approves of these new radiators."

"New Year, I said - A flower unblown; a book unread; a tree with fruit unharvested;
a path untrod; a—— But never mind, never mind."

"Evidently the international situation and the effects of our foreign policy automatically take second place to photographs of the Folies Bergére in your distorted little mind."

"I still think a recording of the London Symphony Orchestra is favourite."

"If the Honourable Members over there will kindly stop playing nap, we'll get down
to this debate on the corporal punishment of adults."

"Be a good boy and eat your black market dinner or you'll never grow up to be famous like Mr. Stanley."

"Mum! I heard Dad tell the man next door that if Gaitskell lets us have petrol for Easter he's going to break the back axle rather than take us to the seaside."

"Well, what are you going to do - fit their lot up with caps or our lot with trilbies?"

"Cheer up, lads - maybe you'll get your snow for Whitsun."

"I see your wife's read about this new Continental fashion for men."

"Save 'em a lot of embarrassment if we pranged 'em before they reach London Docks."

(A Viking ship is on its way to London to commemorate the Danish invasion of England.)

"One wouldn't mind us losing four-and-a-half million pounds if a dozen eggs were a dozen eggs when they arrived."

"Mind you, our old car will still be running when all this new stuff is forgotten.
It'll bloomin' well have to be."

"Algy, I fear Brahms rehearsals and Scottish hospitality are not going to mix."

"If you must pace up and down outside Clarence House smoking all your cigarettes like an expectant father, you can't expect to come home and smoke ours."

"Dad, Georgie bought Lauren Bacall an Easter hat, but she didn't even get off the boat."

"I thought Darwin settled who they are and where they came from."

"Reckon she must have opened your letter to the Express about your
Ideal Landlady being the one next door."

"You realise that if they do ban private cars from cities the cops will have no one to hook except bus drivers and cabbies?"

"This is better than the Guy Fawkes business."

"If I ever lay hands on that little - who said he saw 'em take this road..."

"I see your Old Man's doing his Christmas shopping early this year, Luv."

"How about that - gives you sixpence for doing her shopping and deducts fourpence for speculative gains."

The Giles Family is in America

"That reminds me - I left the light on in the bathroom back home."

"I put it to you that you were driving like a nitwit to run your horse over my client while he was sitting in the road protesting about hunting."

"You wouldn't have kicked up such a fuss about us digging up
half the park if we <u>had</u> found the two million pounds."

"If Vicar's got a Beatle haircut and goes 'Yea, Yea, Yea,' don't forget to squeal."

"Our Vera thought she heard a baby seal calling for help."

"It was your idea taking rejuvenating pills so if your teddy bear's thirsty *you* go and get him a drink of water."

"Dad, I don't think this lady sounds like the Queen."

"That wasn't a nice thing to say about Mrs. Turner's new baby - Some Mothers Do 'ave 'em."

"The Cup Final and Newmarket falling on the same day as our jumble sale was adversary enough, without a certain member of our congregation passing off forged raffle tickets."

"One of my cygnets has just hung a beauty on one of your swans."

"My God - Major Mainwaring, the Club Secretary."

"And now, Miss Smythe, perhaps we might commence dictation?"

"Don't be silly, Florence - no one's going to wrap you up in an iron curtain and send you to Siberia."

"The C.O. tells me he's had a lot of letters from nasty little soldiers who have suddenly discovered they wanted to be engine-drivers since childhood."

"In view of these disappearing aircraft - if anyone asks you if they can borrow
a couple of destroyers, you will come and see me."

"Not a word, Colonel. Remember they're our guests and allies."

"Now if there isn't a war you'll have cleaned all that for nothing."

"The first important lesson in golf is concentration - keeping your eye on the ball..."

"Hundred and one, hundred and two, hundred and three..."

Come, little men - peace for two minutes - 'tis eleven o'clock.

"Are you the one that keeps calling out, 'Good job we've got a Navy'?"

Sport

"Bet you don't chuck <u>his</u> luggage all over the shop!"

"Excuse us just a moment, sir."

"If they were kids you could smack all their behinds and send them to bed."

HIYA-BUD!

Giles goes to Ascot—brings back what the cameramen missed!

"Look! Rita Hayworth."

"Ah, well back to the dress hire shop."

"And that, Clarence, was your cigar on my inflammable handbag."

"It was about time someone thought of a new fashion for men, anyway."

"SH!"

"Do us a favour, boys - let him settle Savold first."

"When you look at the British sports record for recent years, you'll notice how much
we can afford to put the ban on our champions."

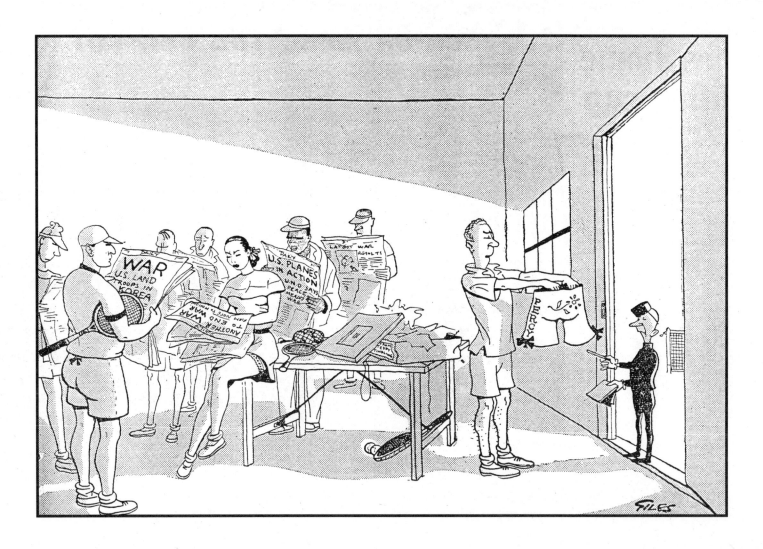

"Bother! Here's me with my nice new embroidered shorts
and Wimbledon not even on the front page."

"If you keep everyone up all night telling them about your past motoring adventures,
you must expect a little sabotage."

"Mum said as you've got a nasty cold through queueing all night for tickets to see Sunderland lose we're not to tell you Rover dug up all your bulbs till tomorrow."

Rationing

"George, this presentation of cigarettes the village made you - is it true you've been selling them at the local for three shillings a packet?"

"Ration what they like, but ration Frankie Sinatra and they'll have ME to reckon with."

"Potato patrol, indeed. I thought we'd finished with this — lark when we finished with the Home Guard."

"Looks like you little old Drones and Spivs'll have to start forming a little old Drones and Spivs' Union."

"How d'you like that - come in here spiv-hunting and walk off with the highest score of the week?"

"That's handy - we've used the last of our petrol getting to the 'Restore the Basic' Rally."

"'A million cups of coffee in Brazil' jars a bit when you've just been told
they're out of beer in the canteen."

"My missus took one look at these 'ere peace plans, then started cleaning me old Home Guard uniform."

Political

"Shameful the way the British are handling this Palestine business."

"If he IS hoarding cigarettes till after the Budget I'm going to laugh
if Dalton puts the price down instead of up."

"Ask yourself a question, Mrs. Harris. Do YOU want another £3,000,000,000 millstone round your neck?"

"I've no doubt we'll find attendance increase considerably with the curtailment of American films in this country."

"The manager says quit this what-are-you-doing-tonight-girls stuff
and start dating a few of 'em up for the Ministry."

"In future, Mrs Jones, everytime you eat a sausage say to yourself, 'Wallop!
There goes another British-owned railway in Buenos Aires.'"

"Somebody heard him whistling 'Red Sails in the Sunset.'"

"Just in case there are any would-be office-boys-to-millionaires among you . . ."

"I don't think you'll get much change out of them, son."

"I reckon we'd all be better off if they ran this Danny Kaye for President."

"O.K. Bud - relax!"

"And if you persist in being late for A.R.P. lectures we have means of helping you to be early."

"Close shave, men! But for the kind Mr. Peron we might have had to
let the British farmers produce beef themselves."

"Well, Clem - what sort of landlady are we going to have?"

"Come on out - we're using it today."

"If you're going to keep pestering me like this I'll take that medal back and not
let you help us win any more wars."

"There you are, Germania; you'll soon be big enough to play with the rough boys on the bomb-site."

(80% of German newspapers released tomorrow will have their original Nazi editors.)

Giles joins the argument - is the Express too up-stage?

"Then when Russia and the States have finished atom-bombing each other <u>we</u> come in with the Home Guard."

"That'll teach you to go telling everybody 'The cuts might have been worse.'"

"I expect we'll have to find a space for his picture in the family album."

GILES, accustomed to being referred to by his friends as a wicked Red, was alarmed at the suggestion in Express Post yesterday that the country is turning Blue because of his humble efforts. He called this special meeting of his staff to discover how all this came about. For the benefit of the uninformed, the gentleman marked with a cross is Giles.

"Now if you send that slogan into the Express and win ten guineas, it'll just about pay your fine."

Campaigners ahoy!

"I should have thought we could pay tribute to President Auriol without you
and Vera dressing like La Belle France."

"Reckon Buck Peron ain't goin' to forget the holes in his hat when two-gun Webb calls for the meat."

"Trust you to leave everything till the last minute."

"Take no notice of 'em Vera - their story about the Russians dropping Colorado beetles on our footballers in Rio is absurd."

"You'd think someone would teach these saboteurs to put their hammer and sickle the right way round."

"I can hardly wait."

A Whitehall Dream . . . on the drive for arms workers.

As if Steel Bills and things were not enough for one week, it is reported that on their way to the House Clem and Herb were confronted by a delegation of bullocks, demanding an enquiry into this nonsense of Webb's about a shortage of slaughter-houses.

"It seems to me that teaching juniors how to make hand-grenades
out of cocoa-tins denotes a Leftish tendency."

"And tell Bevin that gambling's another thing our two countries disagree about."

"Cheero, boys, I'm off - my wife would hate me to be late for Christmas dinner."

"M.P.s' wives - someone let the cat out of the bag about the bar being open during these late sessions."

"I should avoid asking them things like 'What do they think of their first Christmas under a Tory Government?'"

"Even if WE took in exiled kings, I know SOMEONE whose washing would still be hanging out all the week."

"Well, what's the verdict this year - hang the hanging committee? Hang everybody?
Or abolish hanging altogether?"

"Nothing like a week's 'eckling to cheer you up, I always say."

"On my reckoning in about a year we'll all have twenty houses each."

"Best excuse for getting out of doing the garden I've heard -
'They'll probably be building a city on it in 1970'."

"It's still a damn sight better looking than the one we've got next door."

"I don't want to give the impression that there is warfare among pupils and teachers."
TEACHERS' CONFERENCE, BLACKPOOL.

"I, Lord Hill, do promise Mary, never to allow the pornographic Old Testament to be heard on BBC religious programmes."

"Is that the plumber? I think my Grandma has sprung a leak in her Think Tank."

"You've had my vote with your fuel saving, back-to-the-wall campaign, I like me trips to the Polls by Rolls."

"I am not concerned with what is currently popular in the United States, I give everybody three minutes to streak-on cassocks and surplices starting from NOW."

"As a matter of fact I do not think this compensates for missing the opening of the Flat."

"Careful what you spend, dear - third vase back row on your left."

"A charge nurse was demoted this week for less than asking a patient if he could have his guts for garters, nurse."

"How much longer have I got to go on getting our Marriage Minister early morning tea?"

"Cable from her astronaut boy: 'Having a wonderful time, wish you were here.' I suppose floating about in space head over tip with 24 happy rats can be a wonderful time for some people."

"I hope you're not thinking of going to the Conference in that Burton outfit!"

Reynolds News

As the 1930's slid towards war in Europe, and the Spanish Civil War was at its height, Giles was reveling in his first job as a full-time cartoonist at Reynolds News, the left wing Sunday paper owned by the Co-op.

We have selected a few of Giles' cartoons depicting his time at Reynolds News to give you an opportunity to see how his talent to project that unique combination of humour and stoicism shone through at an early stage of his career.

24 October 1937

"Does that fellow have to do that every time?"

"Whats the use trying to run an army now that new pin-table saloon's open?"

"It's about time someone called for this lot, anyhow."

"Honestly - I've never eaten a piece of fish in my life!"

"Are all those British-made?"

"This may be quicker, but personally I prefer the back way!"

"Got a match?"

"Yes, that was my first husband."

"Can you tell me where I can find the
information bureau?"

"And I assure you that he has never been off these premises in his life."

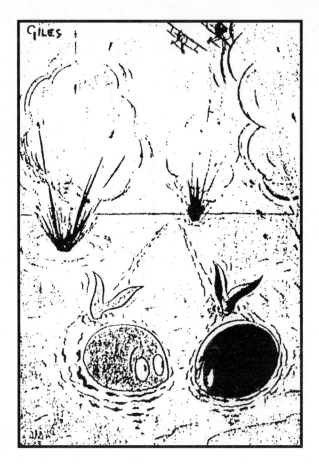

"That's the second time to-day I've been mistaken for a submarine."

FRANCO: Does anyone here understand Spanish?

Dog-racing is by no means a new sport.

"I still say that wing's not meant to flap."

"Where can we get a nice shrimp tea, please?"

"The Sergeant wants to know if anyone here owns the large red sports car outside."

"Merry Christmas, boys!"

"Page Two's Christmas Card."

"What are you doing until next christmas, boys?"

"Auntie Aggie says she's coming to stay for a month,
and would we mind if she brought Cousin Winnie
and her friend?"

"I wonder what Grandpa would have said."

"Mind you, I think it's a pity we all chose the same night."

FOR THE PREMIER'S 70th birthday

"And always remember, we gave them the idea
in the first place."

"It's about time somebody put some traffic lights here."

"We'll keep the fishin' -
You can have the shootin'"

"I'm sure I've seen you two gentlemen before."

"These two gentlemen say they've been robbed, Sarg."

"A chappie was tellin' me there's some horse-racin'
here, as well."

"LAST HAND, you kids, then Scarface'll
read you a fairy story."

The Office Air Raid Rehearsal -

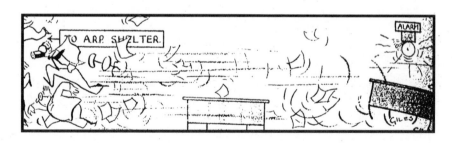

- And the Real Thing

"So you're home for a few days leave?"

"Will honourable English gentlemen please
accept their Howsers?"

"I used up my petrol ration the first day."

"Oh Boy! Oh Boy!! Oh BOY!!!"

"He says he could hear a rattle or something."

"Hello - Making Aeroplanes?"

"Sorry to interrupt - but I've called about your
dog-licence!"

". . . . . And here's a picture of my brother Fred
when he was six!"